FRUITS

BLACKBIRCH PRESS

An imprint of Thomson Gale, a part of The Thomson Corporation

Detroit • New York • San Francisco • San Diego • New Haven, Conn. • Waterville, Maine • London • Munich

Consultant: Kimi Hosoume
Associate Director of GEMS (Great
    Explorations in Math and Science)
Director of PEACHES (Primary
    Explorations for Adults, Children,
    and Educators in Science)
Lawrence Hall of Science
University of California
Berkeley, California

For The Brown Reference Group plc
Editors: John Farndon and Angela Koo
Picture Researcher: Clare Newman
Design Manager: Lynne Ross
Managing Editor: Bridget Giles
Children's Publisher: Anne O'Daly
Production Director: Alastair Gourlay
Editorial Director: Lindsey Lowe

PHOTOGRAPHIC CREDITS
Corbis: Steve Kaufman 13, Tony Wharton/FLPA 16; **NaturePL:** Pete Oxford 4; **Oxford
Scientific Films:** 14; **Photodisc:** PhotoLink 15; **Photos.com:** 1, 5, 7, 10, 18/19, 19t, 20, 21, 22.

Front cover: Photos.com

LIBRARY OF CONGRESS CATALOGING-IN-PUBLICATION DATA

Farndon, John.
   Fruits / [John Farndon].
      p. cm. — (World of plants)
   Includes bibliographical references (p.) and index.
   ISBN 1-4103-0424-8 (lib. : alk. paper)
   1. Fruits (Botany)—Juvenile literature. I. Title

   QK660.F37 2005
   581.4'64—dc22

                                        2005052412

Printed and bound in Thailand
10 9 8 7 6 5 4 3 2 1

Contents

Fruits and plants

Fruits come in many colors, shapes, and sizes. They include oranges, apples, strawberries, and peaches.

▲ Growing fruit

Fruits usually grow out of the middle of a flower, like these passion fruits.

Every plant that grows flowers grows fruit too. On some plants the fruit is tiny and hard, like a nut. On others, it is big, soft, and juicy, like a peach.

When people talk about fruit, they mean just the soft and juicy kind. But scientists mean the hard and dry kind as well. A fruit is the part of a plant where seeds are made.

Seeds begin life in the ovary, where eggs are made in the middle of the flower. As seeds grow, the ovary grows, too. It grows bigger and bigger and becomes the fruit. The fruit surrounds the seeds and protects them.

Ripe fruit

In time, the fruit grows to full size. But it is not ripe yet. That means the seeds inside are not complete. When the seed is ready, the fruit ripens. It changes color. A fruit is often green when it is not ripe. It might then change to red as it ripens. It may also get soft and sweet to eat. Unripe fruits are often tough and taste bitter.

It's Amazing!

People usually think of tomatoes as vegetables. They are really fruits. When a tomato is cut open, small yellow seeds can be seen inside. That means it is a fruit. A tomato is a kind of fruit called a berry. Berries are soft fruits with lots of seeds inside them.

5

All about fruits

Every plant has its own kind of fruit. Some fruits hold just one seed. Other fruits hold lots of seeds.

▼ **Soft fruits**
Here are various kinds of soft fruits, such as drupes and pomes.

Big, soft fruits are called soft, or succulent (juicy), fruits. Apples are soft fruits. So are oranges. But there are lots of different kinds of soft fruits.

A pear is a pome. It has a few small seeds, or pips.

A pomegranate is a berry. It has lots of seeds.

An apple is a pome. It has small seeds, or pips.

A cherry is a drupe. It has one big seed.

A strawberry is not a true berry because its seeds are on the outside.

A soft fruit with one big seed in the middle is a drupe. Plums and cherries are drupes. They usually have soft, sweet flesh and a thin skin. Some soft fruits have seeds in papery cases. They are called pomes. Apples and pears are pomes.

Berries and nuts

Berries are soft fruits with lots of tiny seeds inside. Oranges are berries. So are blueberries and grapes. But a blackberry is not a berry. That is because it is not a single fruit with many seeds. A blackberry is made of lots of tiny drupes, or "drupelets." Each tiny drupe holds one seed. A raspberry is the same.

There are also dry fruits. Dry fruits include nuts, pea pods, and "achenes." Achenes are small dry fruit with just one seed. Ash trees and sycamore trees have achenes.

7

It's Amazing!

Bananas do not grow on trees. Banana plants look like trees, but they are herbs. Banana plants are the biggest herbs in the world. They are the only herbs that grow soft fruit. Bananas are berries. They have lots of seeds. Bananas are green when they are unripe. They only turn yellow when ripe.

Fruits from cool places

Different fruits need different kinds of weather. Some fruits grow well only in places with cool winters, such as North America and Europe. The weather there is called temperate. These fruits are called temperate fruits.

Some temperate fruits grow on trees. Apples, pears, apricots, cherries, nectarines, greengages, peaches, plums, and damsons grow on fruit trees.

Other temperate fruits grow on bushes. Blueberries, cranberries, gooseberries, huckleberries, raspberries, black currants, and red currants all grow on bushes. Strawberries grow on the ground.

Fruit time

Tree fruit like apples and pears first appear in midsummer. They slowly ripen in the sun and are ready to pick by late summer. Bush fruit ripen by midsummer.

Try This!

Did you know you can grow tomatoes from seeds? Ask an adult to buy the seeds in March. Put soil in a plastic cup and spray with water. Push a few seeds into the soil. When leaves appear, fill a large pot outside with soil. Make a cup-sized hole in the soil. Then lift the plant from the cup with its soil and place it in the hole. Add plant food and water regularly. Wait for your tomato to grow.

▶ Temperate fruit

Here are many temperate fruits. Small bush and ground fruits are at the top. Tree fruits are at the bottom.

1. Black currant	6. Mulberry	11. Plums	16. Pear
2. Red currant	7. Sweet cherry	12. Strawberry	17. Apricot
3. Bilberry	8. Gooseberry	13. Damson	18. Peach
4. Blueberry	9. Raspberry	14. Greengage	19. Apple
5. Cranberry	10. Fig	15. Medlar	20. Pear

Fruits from warm places

Some fruits grow well only in warm weather. These fruits grow in places such as Brazil and Colombia, where it stays warm all the time. These places are in the tropics. So the fruits are called tropical fruits. Tropical fruits include bananas, mangoes, melons, and pineapples. Tropical fruits are damaged by cold. Even a light frost will kill them.

Tropical fruits are often much bigger and sweeter than temperate fruits. Melons are often much bigger than a football, and much, much heavier. Jackfruits are big fruits that grow on trees in Southeast Asian forests. A single jackfruit can grow up to 3 feet (1 meter) and can weigh as much as 80 pounds (36 kilograms). That is as heavy as a small adult!

It's Amazing!

Oranges, grapefruits, and lemons are citrus fruits. Citrus fruits contain a mild acid. This acid makes them taste a little sour. But it contains vitamin C, which helps keep people healthy. Oranges are the world's most popular fruit. About 70 million tons of oranges are grown each year. That is about 12 oranges for every man, woman, and child in the world!

1. Pineapple
2. Durian
3. Mango
4. Melon
5. Soursop

6. Persimmon
7. Mangosteen
8. Pomegranate
9. Lychee

10. Akee
11. Banana
12. Guava
13. Kiwi fruit

14. Date
15. Kumquat
16. Tomatillo
17. Custard apple
18. Rambutan

▶ Tropical fruit

Here are many tropical fruits. Most of them grow on trees in tropical forests.

11

Fruits and animals

Plants grow fruit that is good for animals to eat. The animals eat the fruit and spread the seeds.

A big bill for picking fruit.

Fruits are usually soft and tasty. But the seeds inside them are very tough. When animals eat a fruit, the tiny seeds pass through the animals and out with their droppings.

Many kinds of birds eat fruit, especially in warm places like the tropics. In the tropics, fruits are available all year round.

◀ Barred fruit eater

This bird is part of a big family of birds called cotingas. They live in the warm, wet forests of South America. They eat mostly fruit. They have big bills to help them pluck fruits from the trees.

It's Amazing!

Some plants survive best if their seeds are spread by only one kind of animal. The South American hura tree has fruits filled with poison. The poison is so nasty it can burn anyone who even touches the fruits. This puts off most animals. It does not bother a bird called a macaw. It eats the hura fruit. Then it eats a special clay that stops it from getting a stomachache! The macaw spreads the seeds in its droppings.

Birds such as hornbills, toucans, parrots, and tanagers all eat fruit. They have big beaks to help them pull the fruits from the trees. The quetzal of Central America eats avocados. Avocados have very big seeds. After eating the fruit, the quetzal coughs the seed up.

Birds also eat fruit in cooler places such as North America and Europe. Catbirds, mockingbirds, orioles, robins, and waxwings all eat fruit. Fruit in these places is only ripe in fall. For the rest of the year, these birds must find other food to eat, such as insects.

13

Animals that eat fruit

Lots of animals, as well as birds, eat fruit. In the warm, wet forests of South America, many plants rely on bats to eat their fruit and spread their seeds in their droppings. These plants include bananas, peaches, figs, mangoes, and guava.

The bats only drink the fruit's juice. They crush the fruit with their teeth to get the juice. Then they spit out the rest of the fruit. Fruit-eating bats have good eyes and a good sense of smell. These senses help bats find fruit at night.

In tropical forests other big animals eat fruit, too. Some animals climb up and pick the fruit straight from the trees. Monkeys, sloths, and kinkajous can all do this. Other animals like deer wait until the fruit falls to the ground.

Plants need animals to eat their fruit only when the seeds inside are ready. So the fruit tastes sour until it is ripe. It then changes color and becomes soft and sweet. Monkeys are fussy eaters. They only choose the fruit that has just turned ripe.

◀ Blackberry feast

Blackberries are only ripe in fall. At that time of year, wood mice fill themselves up with fruit until they get very fat. The fat keeps the mice alive when they are sleeping through the winter.

It's Amazing!

The durian fruit grows in Southeast Asia. Animals know when it is ripe by its smell. This smell is so strong that people can smell it half a mile (0.7 kilometers) away. The ripe fruit smells like rotting fish. But forest animals know there is a treat in store. When they smell the ripe fruit, bears squirrels, orangutans, and even tigers flock to the tree to eat the delicious fruit.

Insects and fruits

Many insects use fruits in different ways. Some eat them. Some live in them. Some lay their eggs in them. Some even use fruits as nurseries for their young.

Most flies feed on fruit. Flies have strawlike mouthparts. They sip the sweet juice of fruit. Fruit flies especially like fruit.

Fruit flies like fruit best when it is very ripe or even rotting. That is when the fruit is sweetest. Fruit flies also lay their eggs in fruit on trees. The eggs hatch into maggots. The maggots dig through the fruit, eating it. Maggots turn into adult flies after the fruit has fallen to the ground.

★ It's Amazing! ★

These red lumps on oak trees look like fruit. They are even called oak apples. But they are not fruit at all. They are growths called galls. Galls grow around places where some insects lay their eggs. Oak apples grow on oak leaves, twigs, or bark. They are made by the eggs of insects called cynipid wasps.

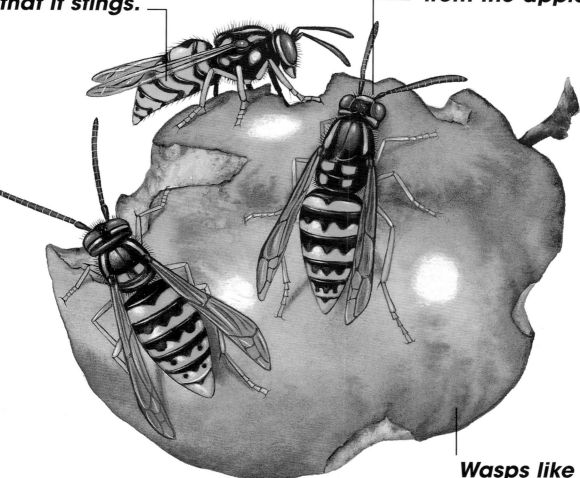

A wasp's bright yellow body warns that it stings.

The wasps suck sweet juice from the apple.

Wasps like bruised and rotting fruit because it is sweeter than fresh fruit.

▲ Adult wasps on apple

Young wasps are meat eaters. They feed on caterpillars and other insects. Adult wasps are vegetarian. They live on fruit and the sweet nectar of flowers.

Fruits and people

Most people eat a lot of fruit. Fruit is very tasty and sweet. It is also full of good things that keep people healthy.

All around the world, people grow fruit to eat. In cool parts of the world, fruits like apples, pears, and cherries are grown in places called orchards. In warmer places, fruit such as oranges and lemons are grown in places called groves. In very warm places, tropical fruits such as bananas are grown in places called plantations.

Fruit for health

Fruit is very healthy food to eat. It contains sugars that are good for energy, especially fruit like bananas.

Fruit contains vitamins, too. The body needs different kinds of vitamins to stay fit. Most fruit has vitamins called A and B.

▶ Fruit market

Red and green apples, yellow pears, red peaches, and oranges make a colorful display at a fruit stall.

Vitamin A is good for the skin, eyes, and lungs. Vitamin B keeps muscles strong and gives your body energy. It helps children grow, too. Oranges, lemons, tomatoes, and strawberries all contain a vitamin called vitamin C. Vitamin C helps the body fight colds and other illnesses.

✦ It's Amazing! ✦

Fruit starts to go bad as soon as it is picked. So it must be eaten right away or preserved (kept fresh). Fruit can be preserved in many ways. Some is dried in the sun, like the chilies here. Some is put into cans. Some is blasted with icy gases to chill it. Most fruit in supermarkets is chilled like that. It means fruit can come from far away because it stays fresh on the journey. It also means you can eat fresh fruit at any time of year.

Fruit juice

▼ Bunch of grapes

People have been making wine from grape juice for hundreds of years.

Fruit is not just for eating. It can be turned into drinks, too. Most soft fruits can be squeezed to make juice. These include apples, pineapples, mangoes, tomatoes, and lemons.

Almost half the oranges grown in the world are used to make orange juice. Oranges are put in huge machines that squeeze out the juice. The juice is chilled to stop it from going bad, then put in cartons and bottles. Water is usually added to make the juice go farther.

Lemonade is a drink made from the juice of lemons. Many people still make it at home. They heat the juice with water and plenty of sugar to take away the bitter taste of lemons. After it is chilled, lemonade is a refreshing summer drink.

Fruit for wine

Another well-known drink made from fruit is wine. Wine is made from grape juice. Grapes are the fruit of vines. Vines grow well only in warm, sunny places, like California. Vines grown for their grapes are planted in vineyards.

It's Amazing!

Like grapes, olive trees grow only in warm places like California and around the Mediterranean. Some olives are crushed and made into oil for salads or cooking. Some olives are eaten whole. Olives are not sweet, but they are tasty. They can be preserved in oil or salty water. Sometimes the pits are pushed out. Then the olives may be stuffed with red chilies, as shown above.

Fruits with meaning

Fruits often have special meanings for people. The bilva fruit looks like a big red-brown apple. For Buddhists, it means doing the right thing—the thing that bears fruit.

For Chinese people, a pomegranate is a sign a woman will have many children. If a young woman is given a longan fruit, the Chinese say she will have clever children.

◀ Bad apple
This stained-glass window shows Eve giving Adam an apple. In the Bible, Adam and Eve were the first people. They lived in the Garden of Eden. But they were driven out by God when they were tricked into eating an apple from the Tree of Knowledge.

Glossary

achene a type of small dry fruit with just one seed.

berry a soft fruit with lots of seeds inside, like a blueberry.

drupe a soft fruit with one big seed in the middle, like a cherry.

drupelet a tiny drupe that is joined to others to make a bigger fruit, like a blackberry.

fruit the part of a plant that contains its seeds.

gall a growth on a plant made by insects for their eggs.

pome a soft fruit with seeds in papery cases in the middle, like an apple or a pear.

ripe when a fruit and the seed inside are fully grown and ready to be eaten.

succulent fruit a big, very soft, juicy fruit.

temperate fruit a fruit that grows in a place where the weather is normally mild, like the United States and Europe.

tropical fruit a fruit that grows in a place where the weather is warm or hot all the time, like the Amazon forest of South America.

23

Find out more

Books

Sally Morgan. *Flowers, Fruits and Seeds.* New York: Chrysalis, 2004.

Charles Micucci. *Life & Times Of The Apple.* New York: Orchard Paperbacks, 1992.

Web sites

The Great Plant Escape

www.urbanext.uiuc.edu/gpe

Kids Valley Garden

www.raw-connections.com/garden

Index